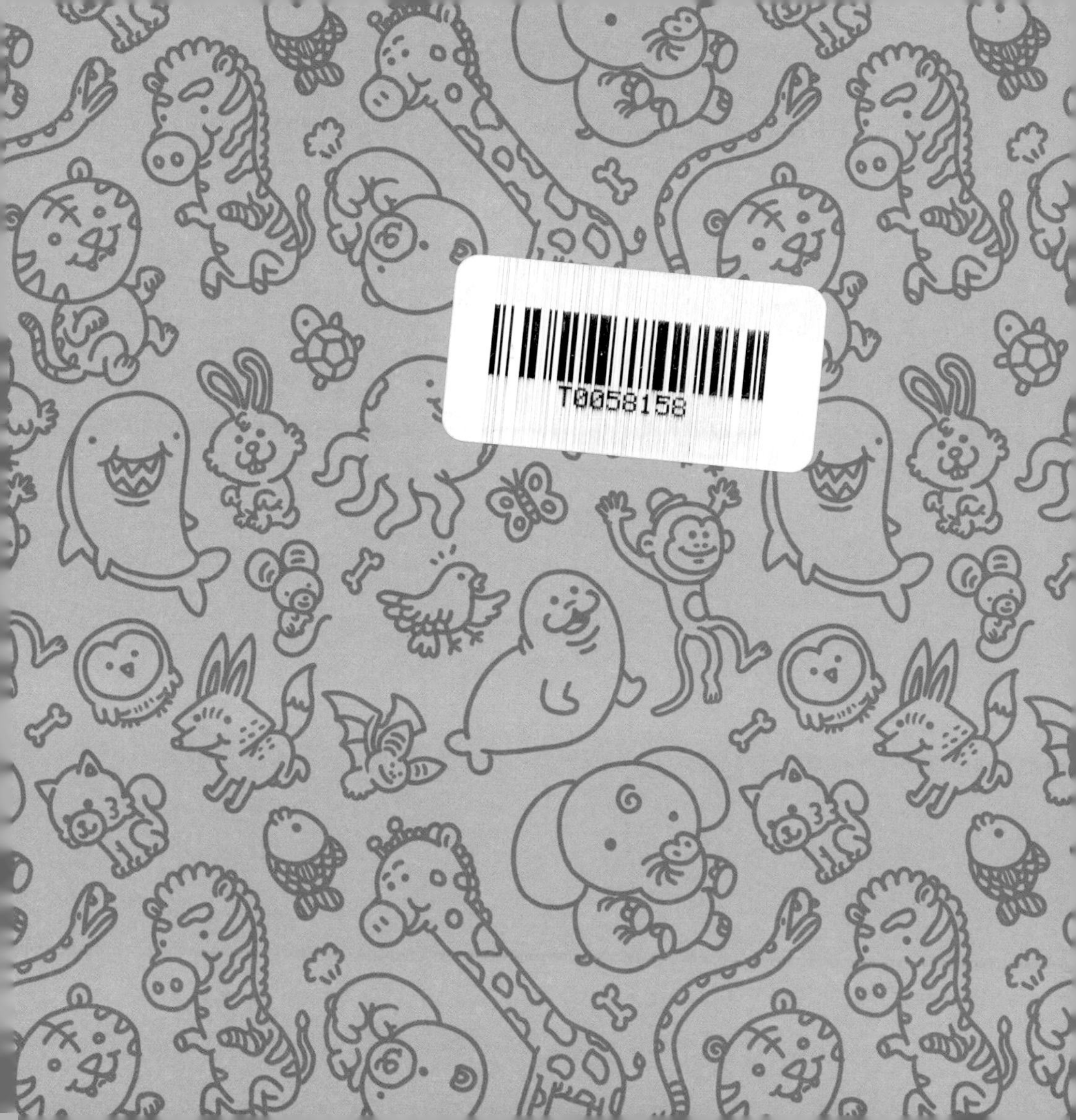

# THE Adorable
# CIRCLE OF LIFE

Skyhorse Publishing books may be purchased in bulk at special discounts for sales promotion, corporate gifts, fund-raising, or educational purposes. Special editions can also be created to specifications. For details, contact the Special Sales Department, Skyhorse Publishing, 307 West 36th Street, 11th Floor, New York, NY 10018 or info@skyhorsepublishing.com.

Skyhorse® and Skyhorse Publishing® are registered trademarks of Skyhorse Publishing, Inc.®, a Delaware corporation.

Visit our website at www.skyhorsepublishing.com.

10 9 8 7 6 5 4 3 2 1

Library of Congress Cataloging-in-Publication Data is available on file.

Cover illustrations by Alex Solis
Cover design by Brian Peterson

Print ISBN: 978-1-5107-1575-2
Ebook ISBN: 978-1-5107-1577-6

Printed in China

# THE Adorable
# CIRCLE OF LIFE

*A Cute Celebration of Savage Predators and Their Hopeless Prey*

## Alex Solis

Skyhorse Publishing

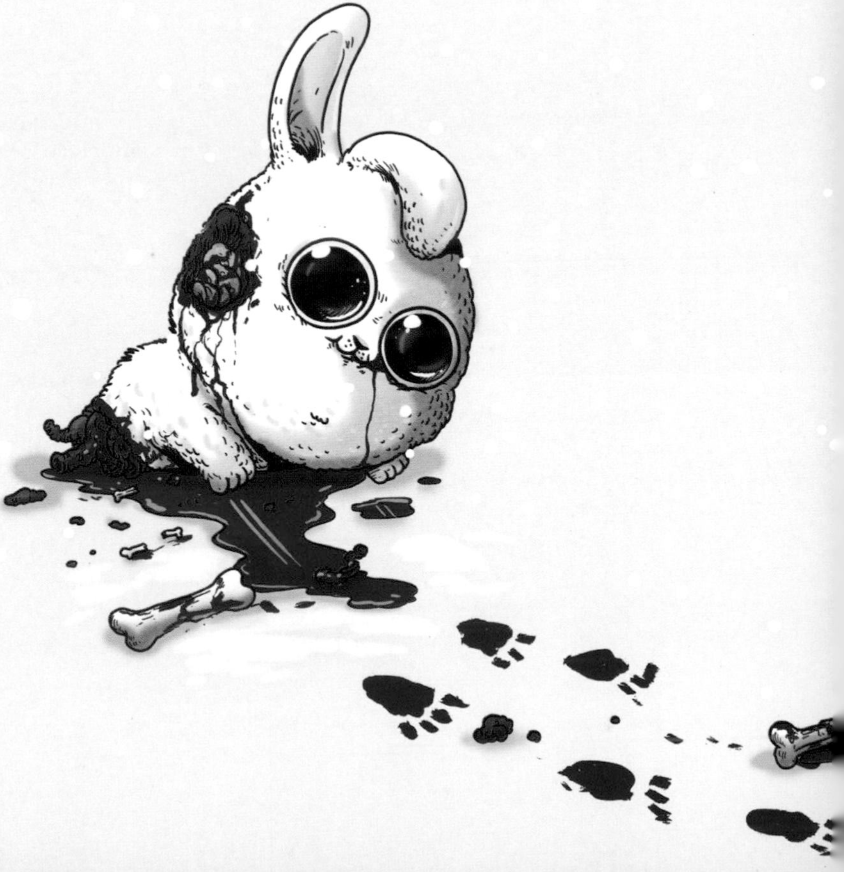

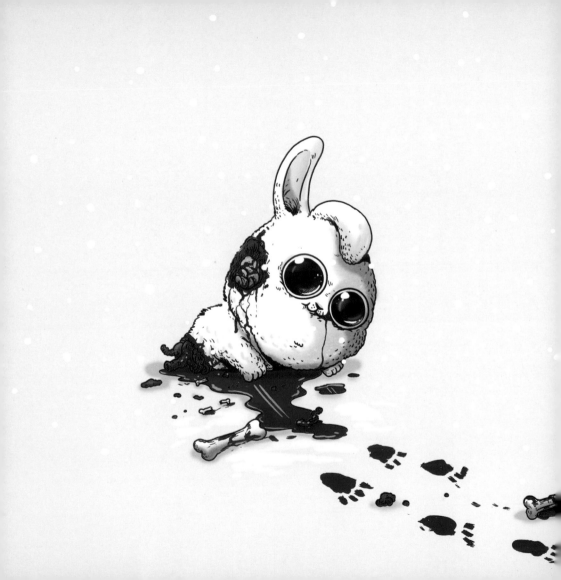

# INTRODUCTION

*Savage. Menacing. Ruthless. Predators get a pretty bad rap. Sure, they prey on helpless animals that never stand a chance. But behind those jagged teeth, powerful jaws, and razor-sharp claws, every predator has a softer side. Maybe even an adorable one.*

*Everyone has compassion for the cute bunny or lamb. But what about their predators who are working hard for their meal? Capturing their prey is life or death for them. Just think about the last time you had to hunt for food while hangry. You can understand, right?*

*It's time to give the predators a break. Because in the end, both predators and their prey play a role. Let's celebrate all animals who complete The Adorable Circle of Life.*

"Until the lion tells his side of the story,
the tale of the hunt will always glorify the hunter."
        —Zimbabwean Proverb

"Eagles may soar, but weasels don't get sucked into jet engines."

—John Benfield

"We can't stop here, this is bat country!"

—Hunter S. Thompson, *Fear and Loathing in Las Vegas*

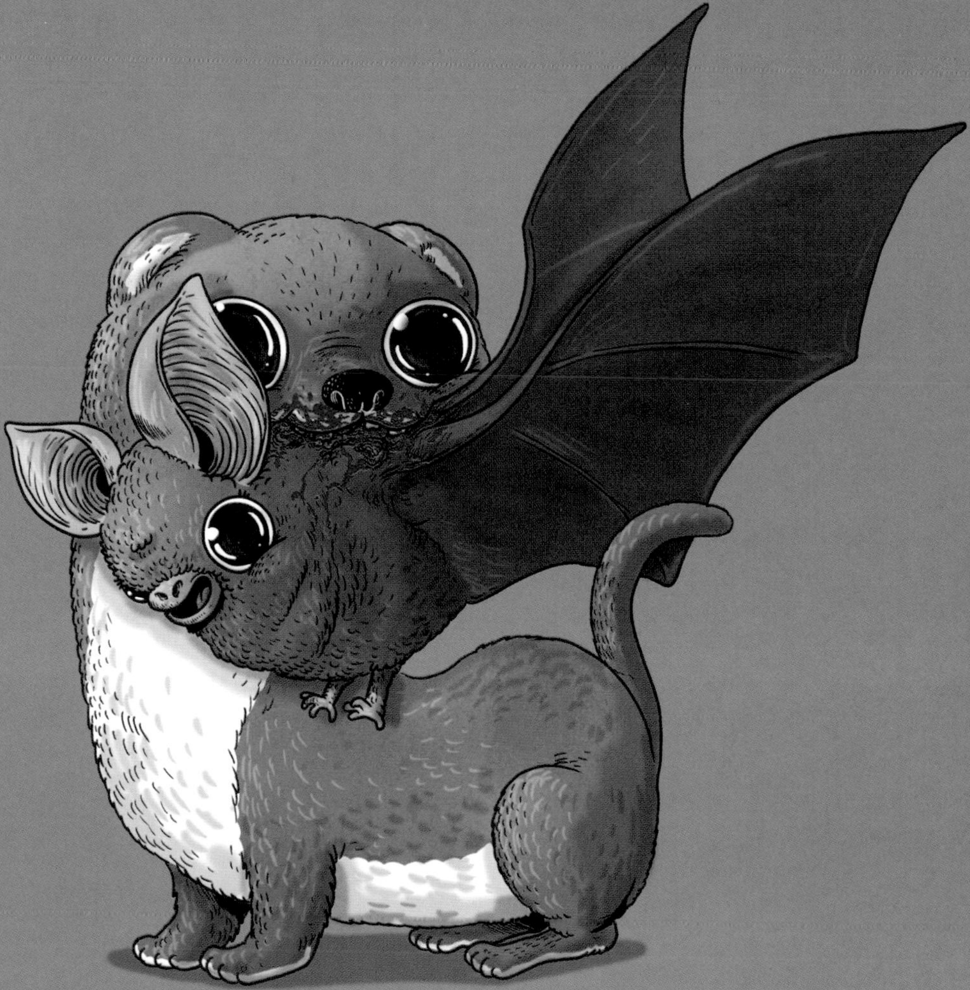

"Blaming the wolf would not help the sheep much.
The sheep must learn not to fall in the clutches of the wolf."
　　　　—Mahatma Gandhi

"We split from our common ancestor with the octopus  half a billion years ago. And yet, you can make friends with an octopus."

—Sy Montgomery

"When Mary is confused or perplexed, she spurts anger the way an octopus spurts ink, and hides in the dark cloud of it."

—John Steinbeck, *The Winter of Our Discontent*

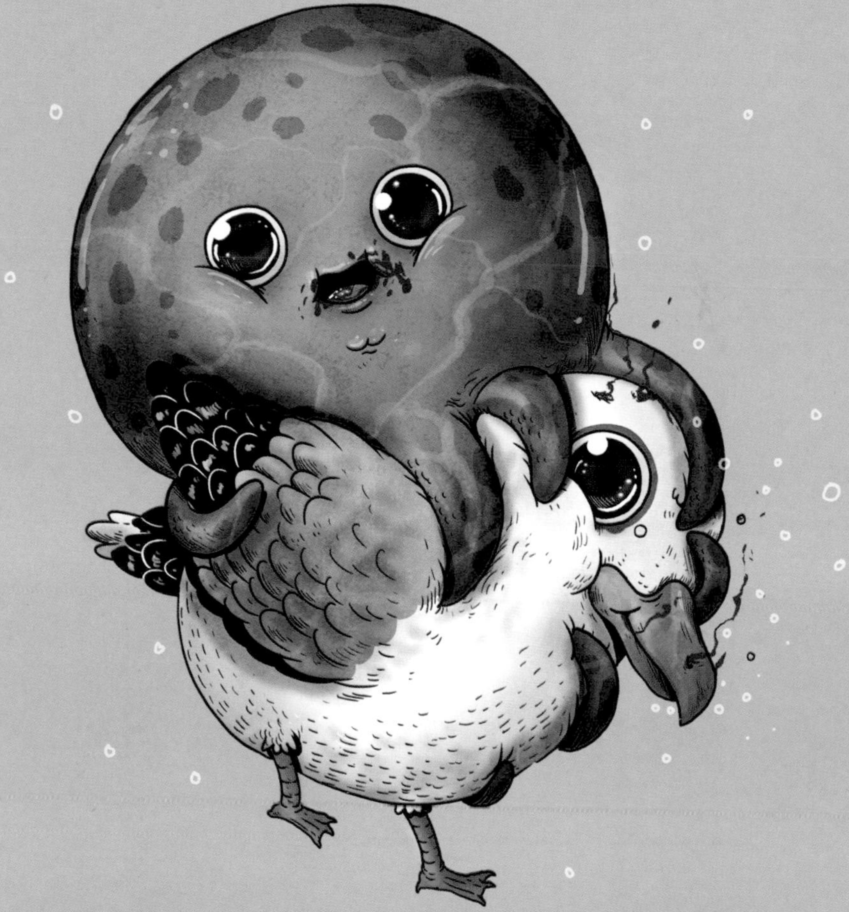

"For my own part, I wish the bald eagle had not been chosen the representative of our country. He is a bird of bad moral character. He does not get his living honestly."

—Benjamin Franklin

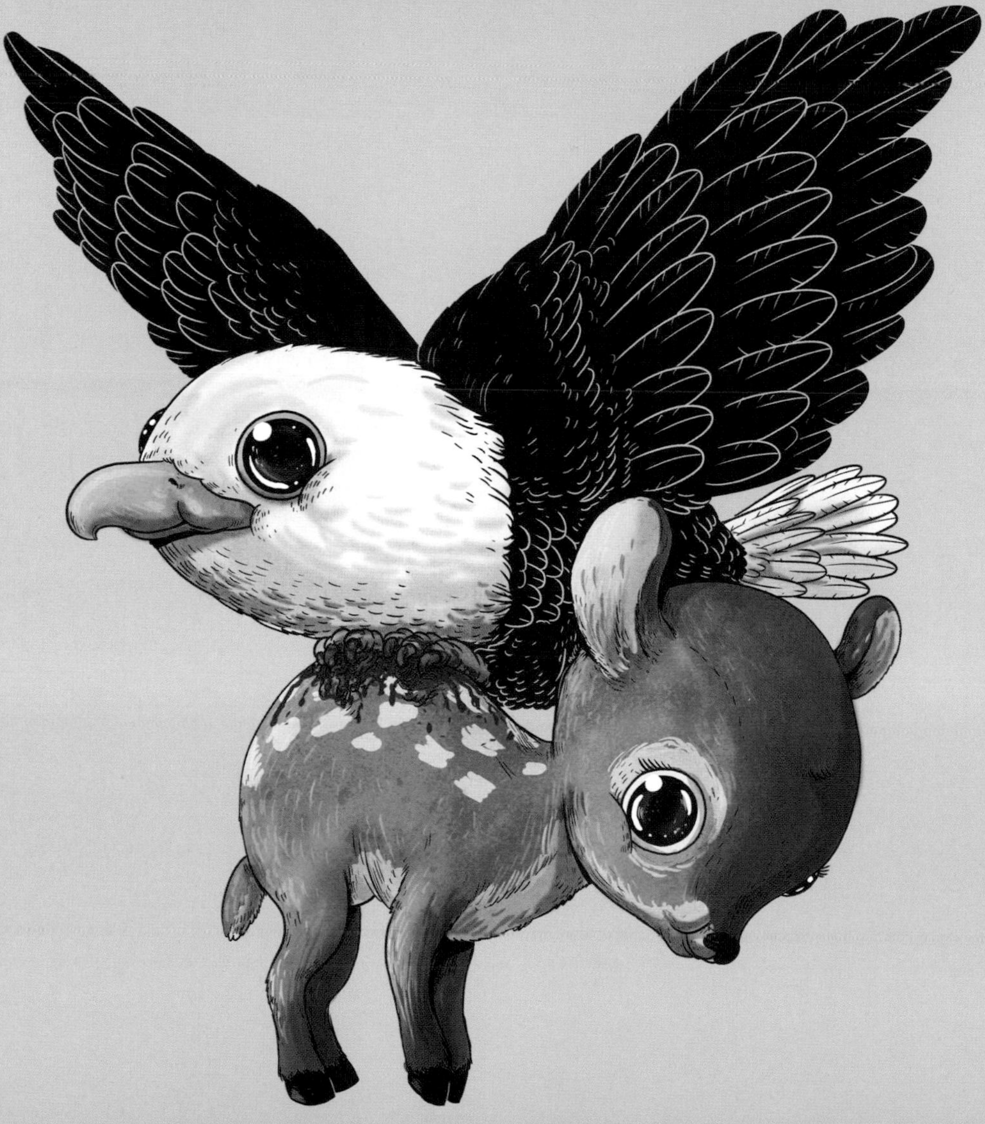

"A fly is as untamable as a hyena."
　　　　—Ralph Waldo Emerson


"When you have got an elephant by the hind legs and he is trying to run away, it's best to let him run."
　　　　—Abraham Lincoln

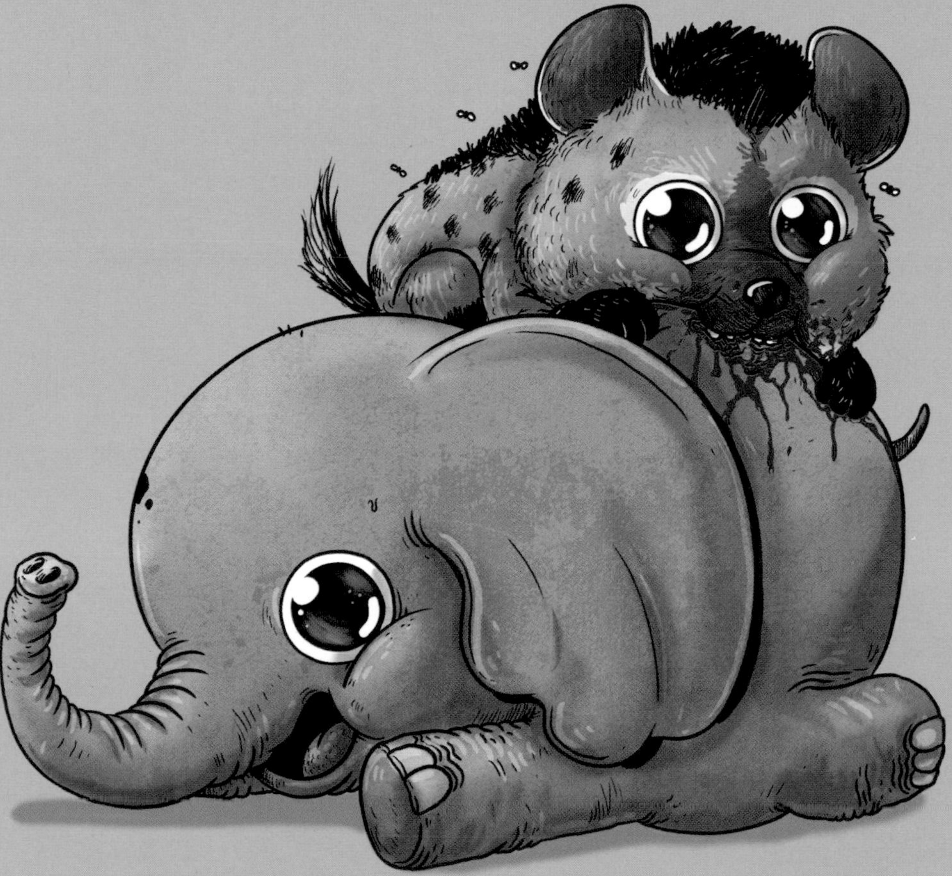

"An appeaser is one who feeds a crocodile,
hoping it will eat him last."
   —Winston Churchill


"The poor monkey, quietly seated on the ground,
seemed to be in sore trouble at this display of anger."
   —Henry Walter Bates

"Never wound a snake; kill it."
>       —Harriet Tubman


"Some persons think that they have to look like a hedgehog to be pious."
>       —Billy Sunday

"The tigers have found me and I do not care."
                    —Charles Bukowski

"We were restless for ages . . . After a while I heard an owl
hooting and calmed myself by thinking of it flying over
the dark fields – and then I remembered it would be pouncing on mice.
I love owls, but I wish God had made them vegetarian."
   —Dodie Smith

"The reason cats climb is so that they can look down
on almost every other animal—
it's also the reason they hate birds."
　　　　　—K. C. Buffington

"The stronger the color red is on the ladybug, the better your luck will be."
                    —Author Unknown

"All I know is, it is better to be the whale than the squid."
    —Roger Ebert

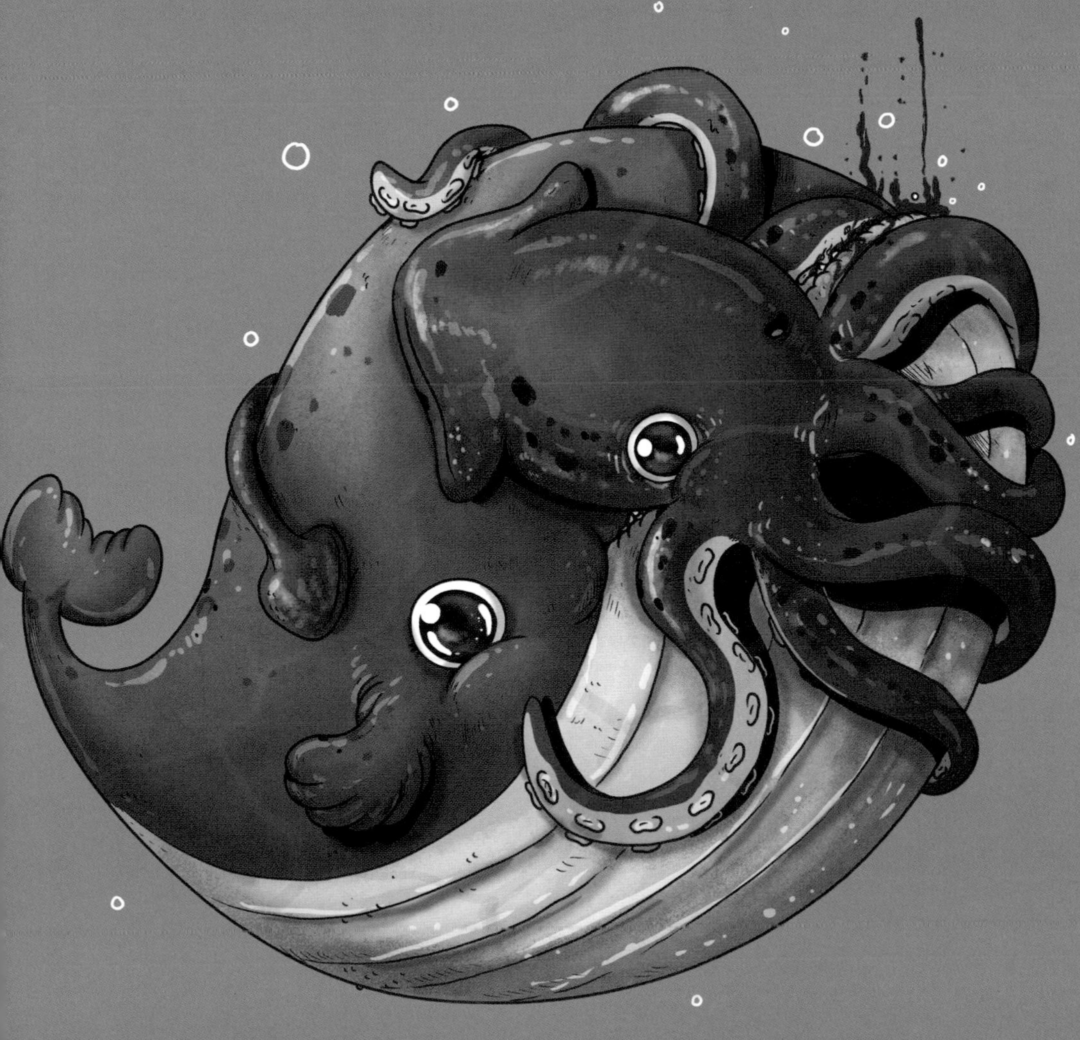

"Is a hippopotamus a hippopotamus,
or just a really cool Opotamus?"
—Mitch Hedberg

"A man looking at a hippopotamus may sometimes be tempted
to regard a hippopotamus as an enormous mistake."
—G. K. Chesterton, *Charles Dickens*

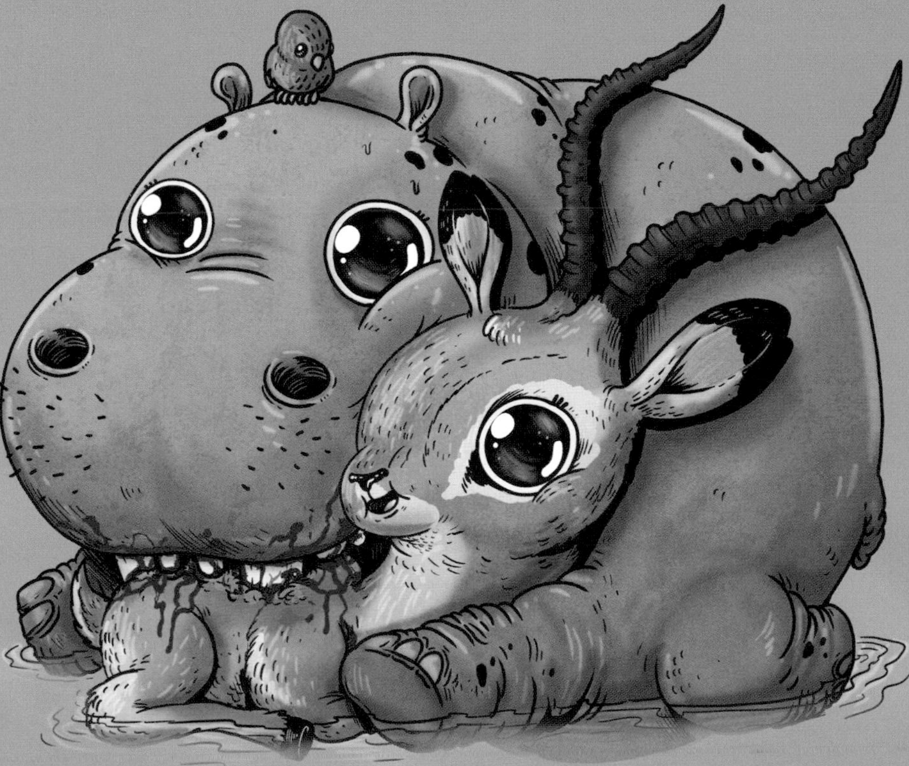

"When the fox hears the rabbit scream
he comes running, but not to help."

—Thomas Harris, *Hannibal*

"When the Coyote falls, he gets up and brushes himself off; it's preservation of dignity. He's humiliated, and it worries him when he ends up looking like an accordion. A Coyote isn't much, but it's better than being an accordion."

—Chuck Jones, *Conversations*

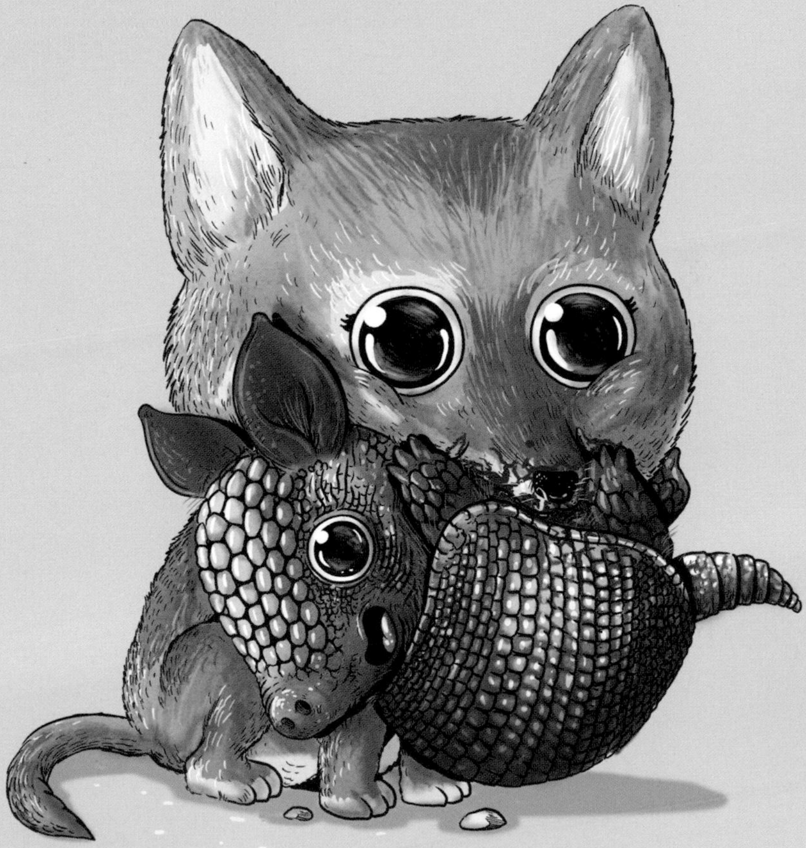

"There's no question dolphins are smarter
than humans as they play more."
                    —Albert Einstein


"Dolphins: Animals that are so intelligent that, within a
few weeks of captivity, they can train a man to stand on
the edge of their pool and throw them food three times a day."
                    —Hal Roach

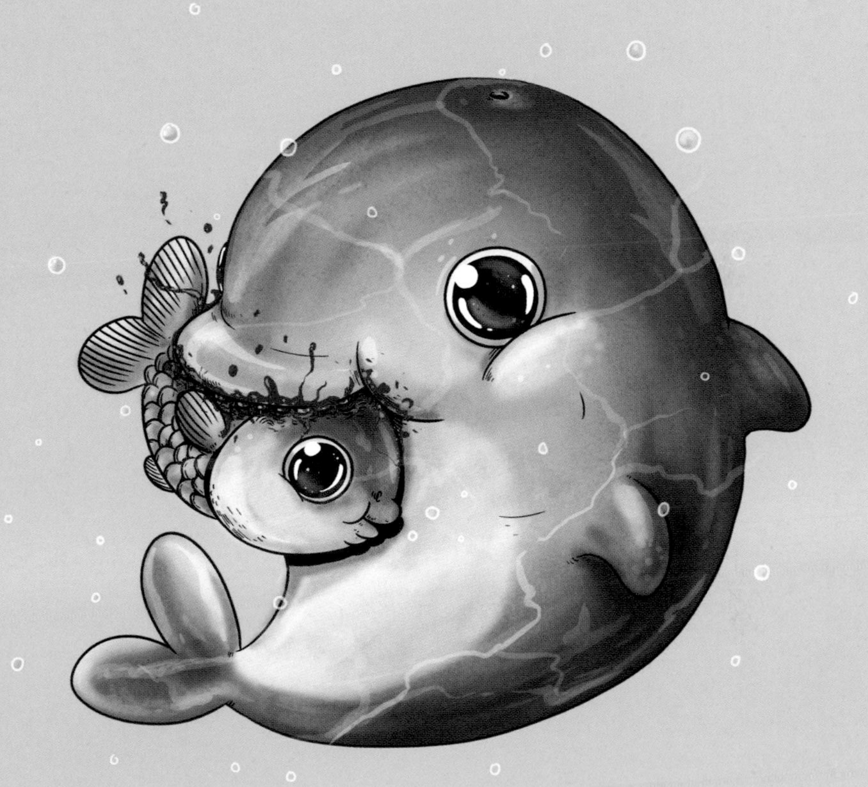

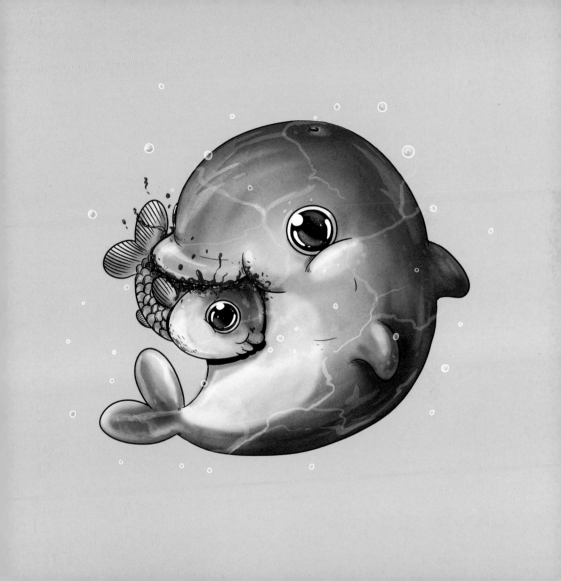

"You do not ask a tame seagull why it needs to disappear from time to time toward the open sea. It goes, that's all."
        —Bernard Moitessier


"Try to be like the turtle—at ease in your own shell."
        —Bill Copeland

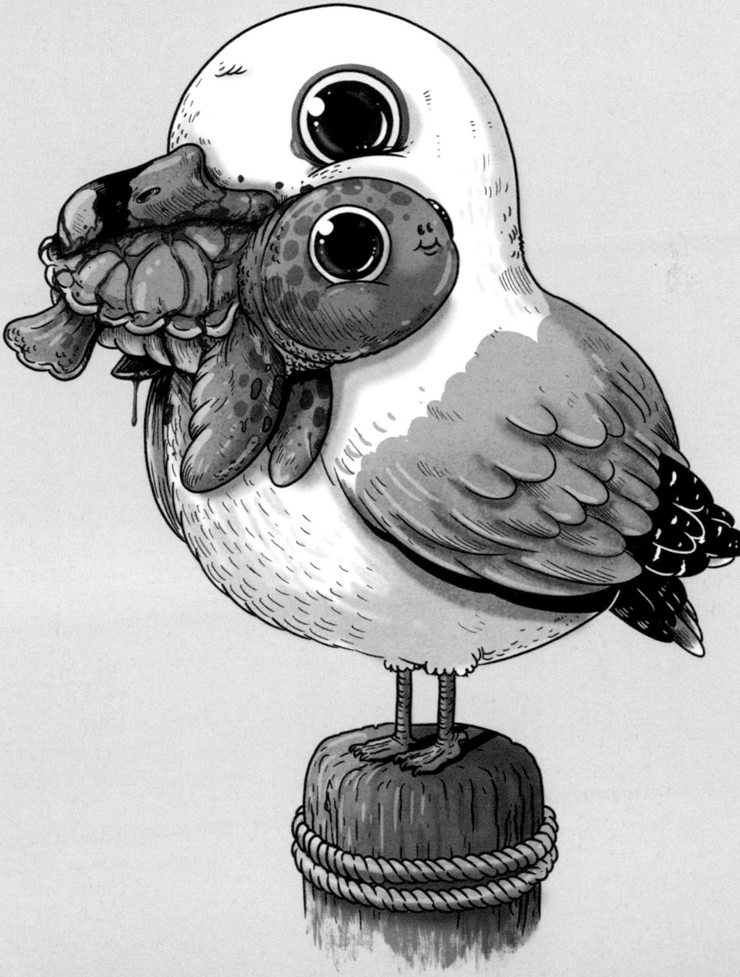

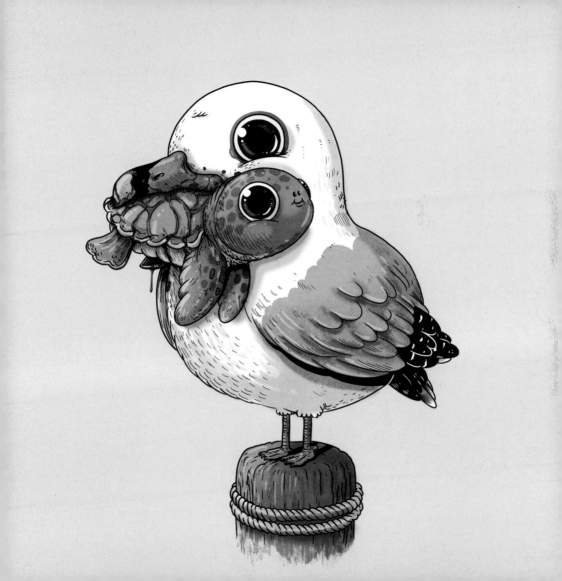

"Do not count your chickens before they are hatched."
        —Aesop


"The key to everything is patience. You get the chicken by hatching the egg, not by smashing it."
        —Arnold H. Glasow

"Even as I speak, the very last polar bear may be dying of hunger on account of climate change, on account of us. And I sure miss the polar bears. Their babies are so warm and cuddly and trusting, just like ours."

—Kurt Vonnegut Jr., *Armageddon in Retrospect*

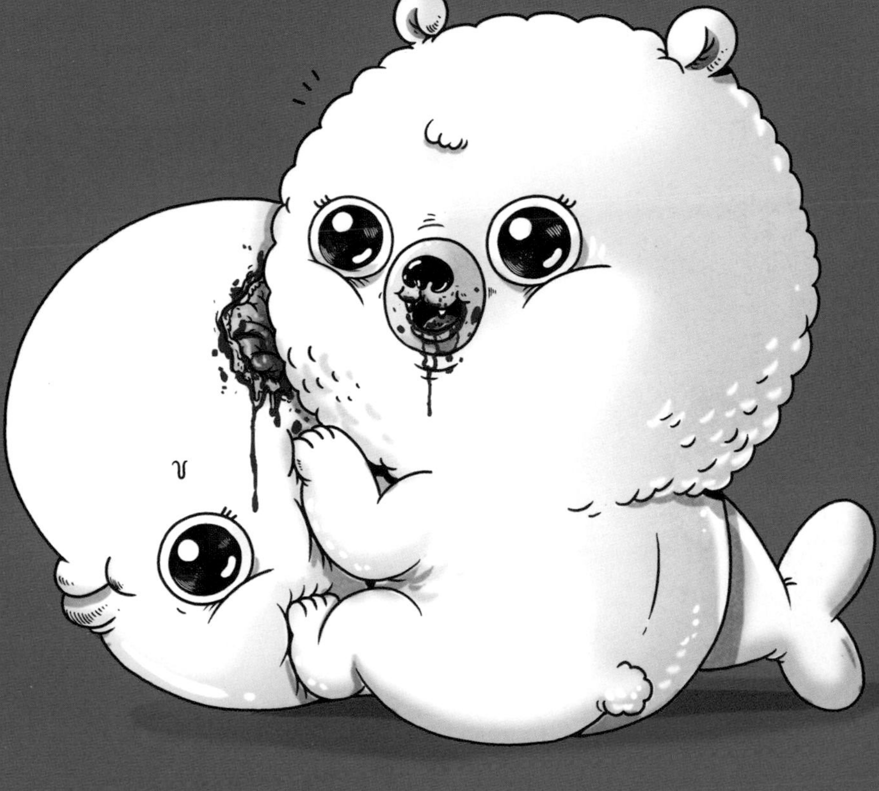

"Many people continue to think of sharks as man-eating beasts. Sharks are enormously powerful and wild creatures, but you're more likely to be killed by your kitchen toaster than a shark!"

—Ted Danson

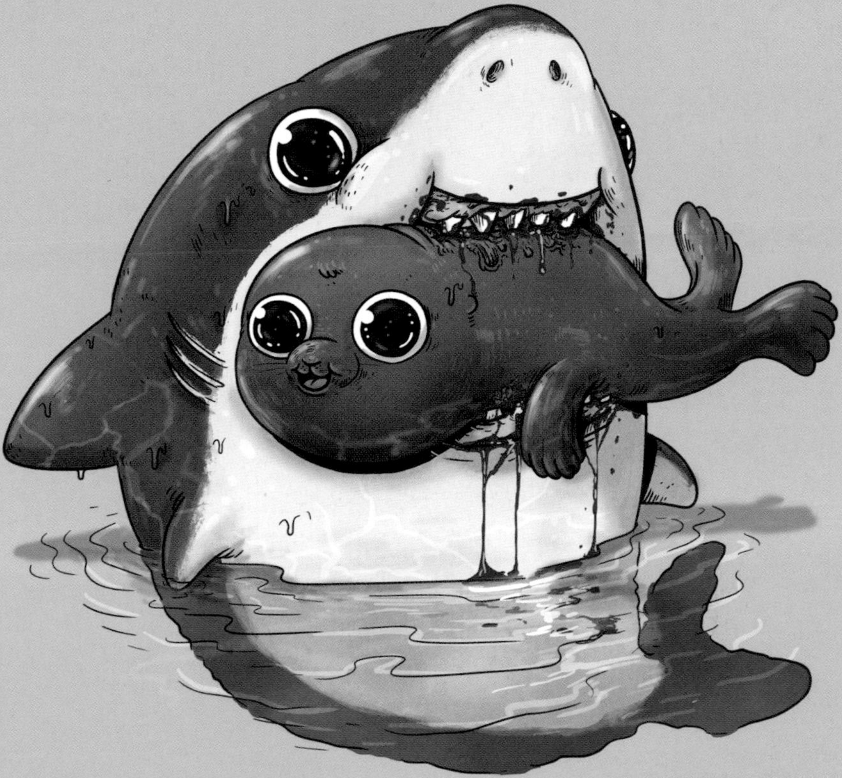

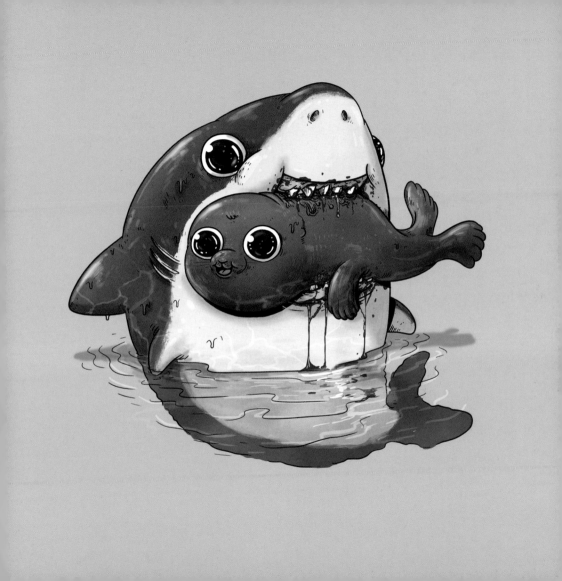

"It's an incredibly difficult thing to bring a giraffe down. They can kill a lion with a single blow from their feet."
        —Joanna Lumley


"God is really only another artist. He invented the giraffe, the elephant, and the cat. He has no real style, He just goes on trying other things."
        —Pablo Picasso

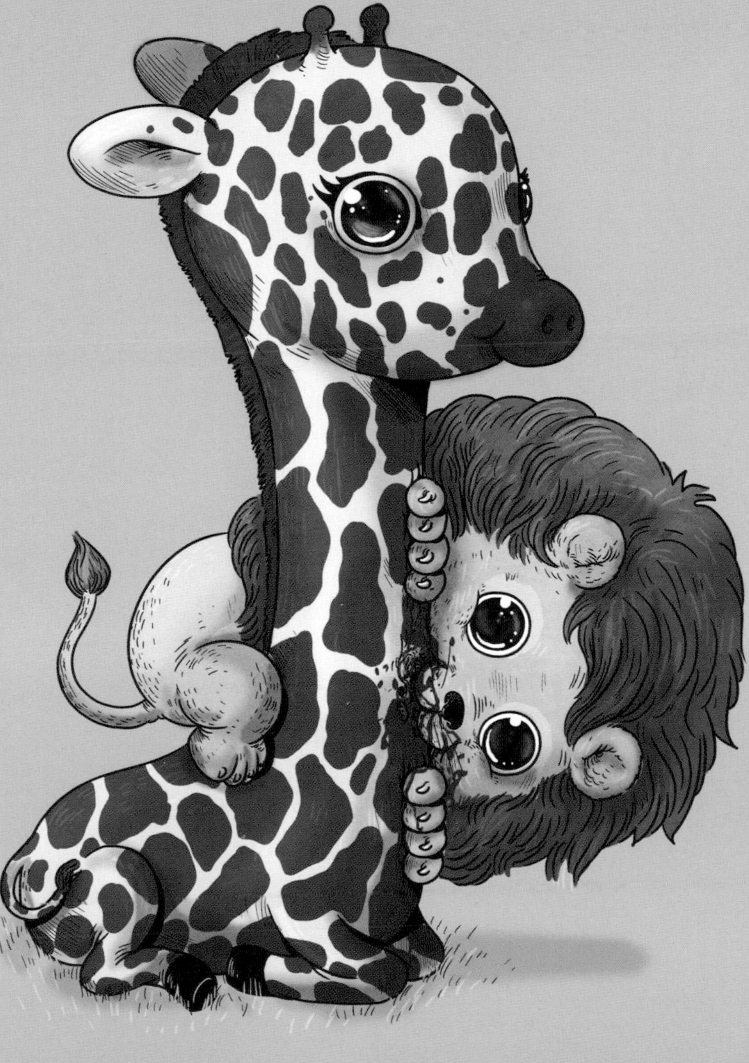

"The mongoose I want under the stairs when the snakes slither by."

—Hannibal Lector, *Hannibal*

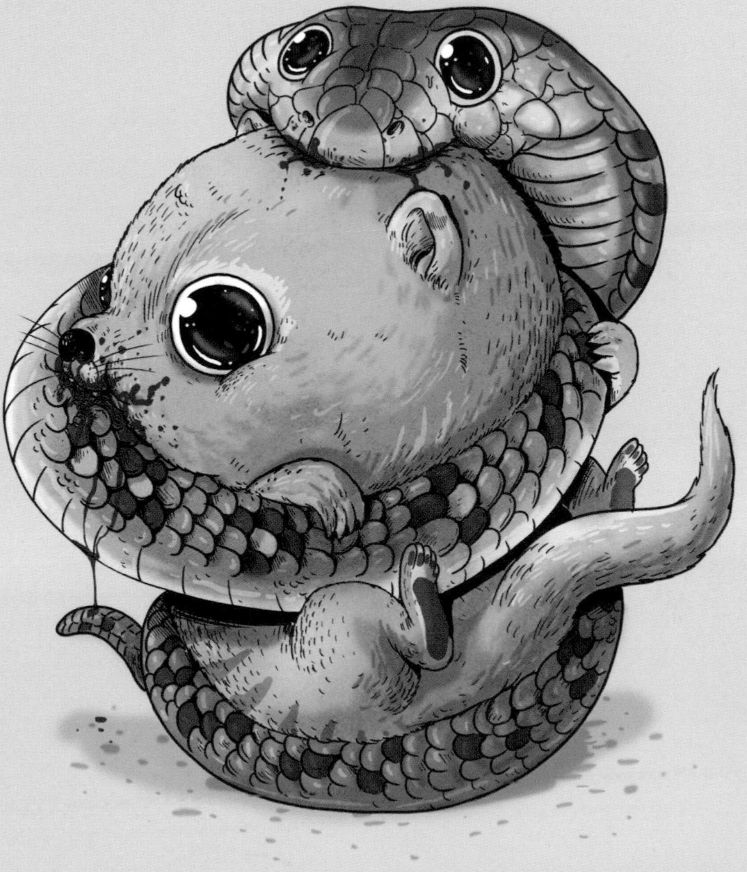

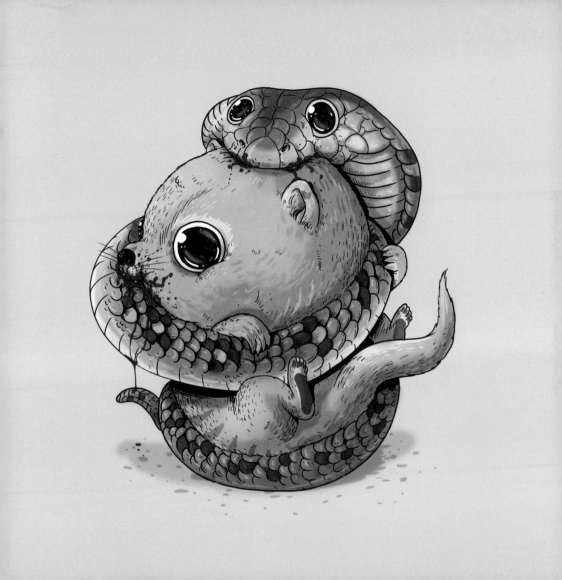

"How daintily the butterfly  Flits to the spider's lace
Entranced by glimm'ring silver strings Entwined with glist'ning grace.
How craftily the spider speaks And whispers, 'All is well,'
Caresses it with poison'd feet And sucks it to a shell"

—Heather Dixon, *Entwined*


"Butterflies are the heaven sent kisses of an angel."
—Author Unknown

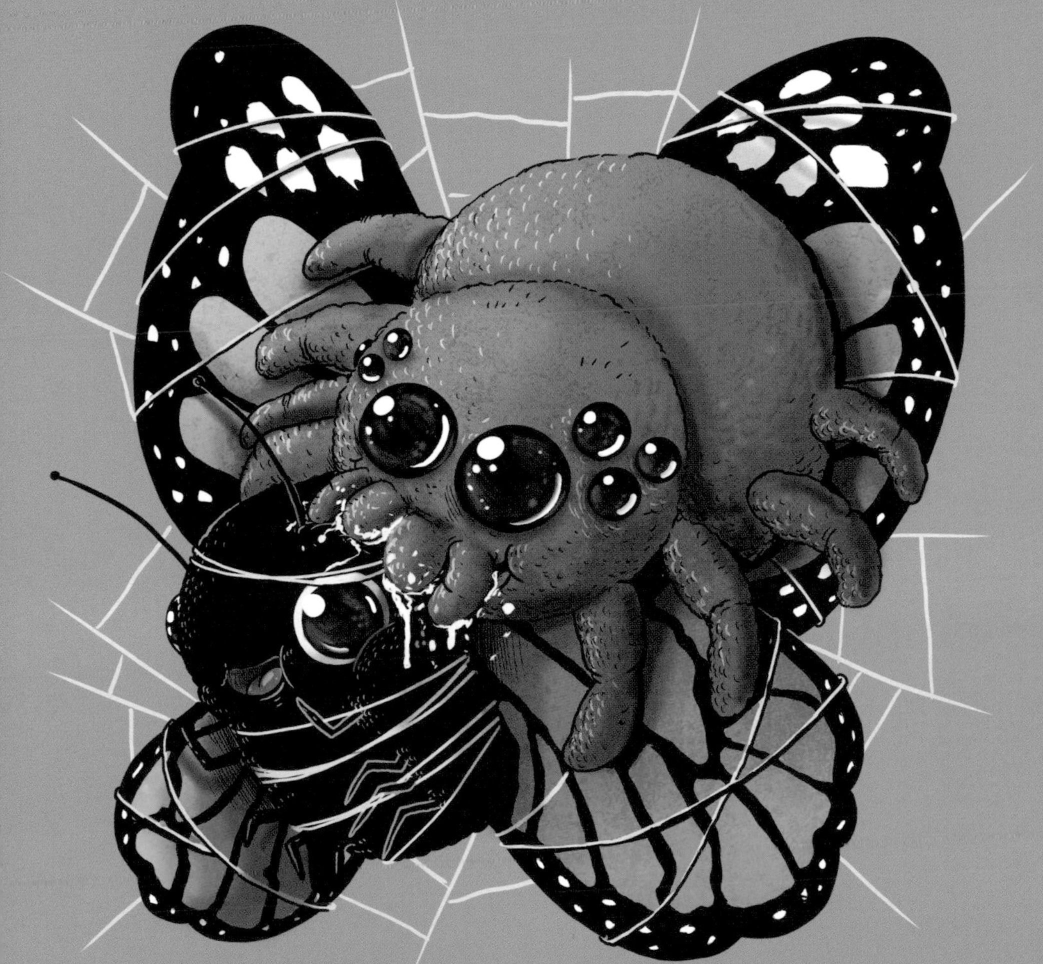

"The penguin doesn't know it's cute, and the leopard seal doesn't know it's kind of big and monstrous. This is just the food chain unfolding."

—Paul Nicklen

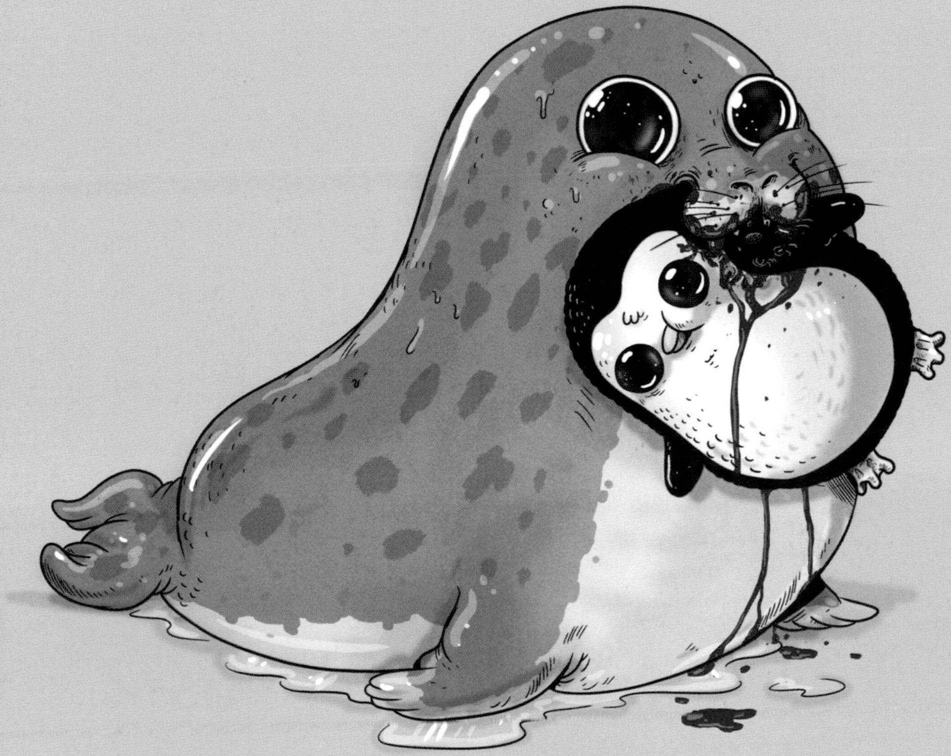

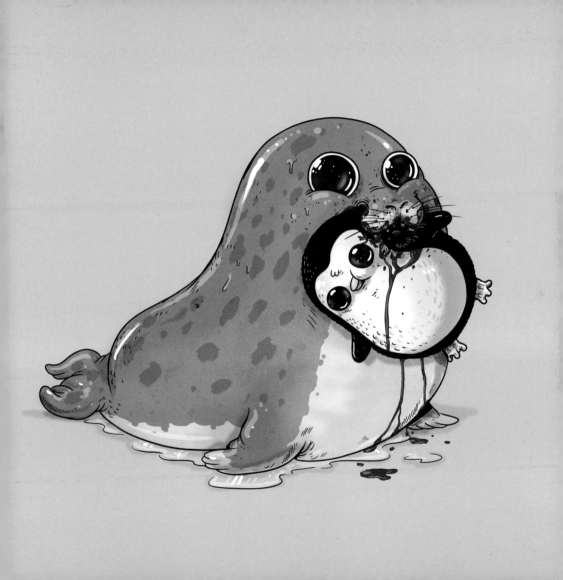

"In the third month, the sun rising,
the Boar and the Leopard on the field of Mars to fight;
The tired Leopard raises its eye to the heavens,
sees an eagle playing around the sun."
    —Nostradamus

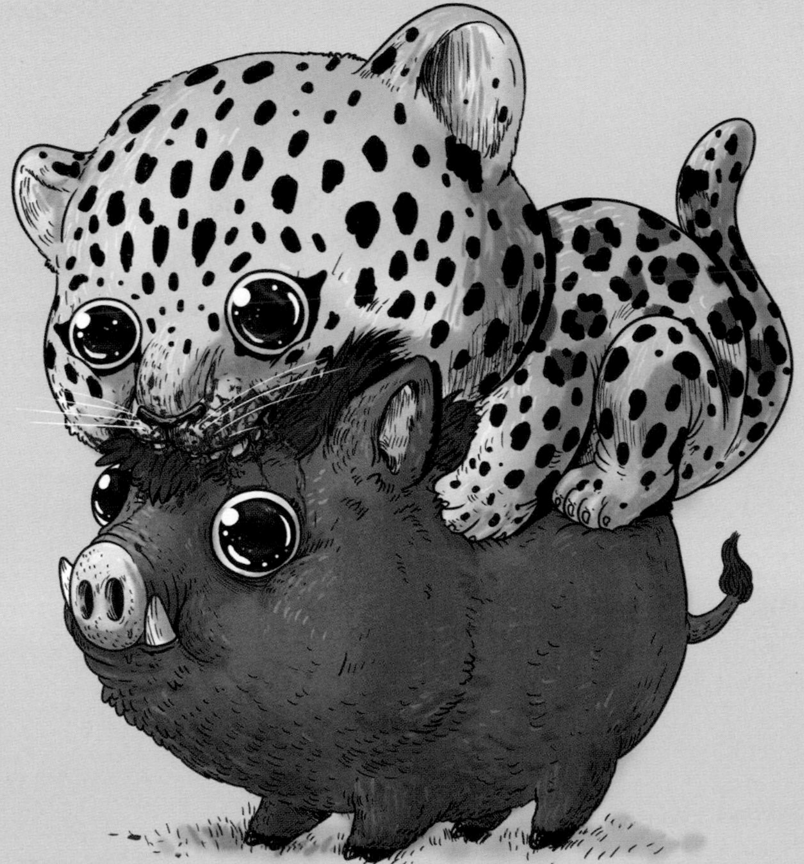

"Yet otters have not been hunters in water long enough for the habit to become an instinct."
—Henry Williamson

"It's not easy being green."
—Kermit the Frog

"When birds burp, it must taste like bugs."

— Bill Watterson, *Calvin and Hobbes*

"Self-love for ever creeps out, like a snake,
to sting anything which happens to stumble upon it."
　　　—Lord Byron


"Snake looks scary for us and we look scary for the snake!
Always try to see yourself from the eyes of others!"
　　　—Mehmet Murat İldan

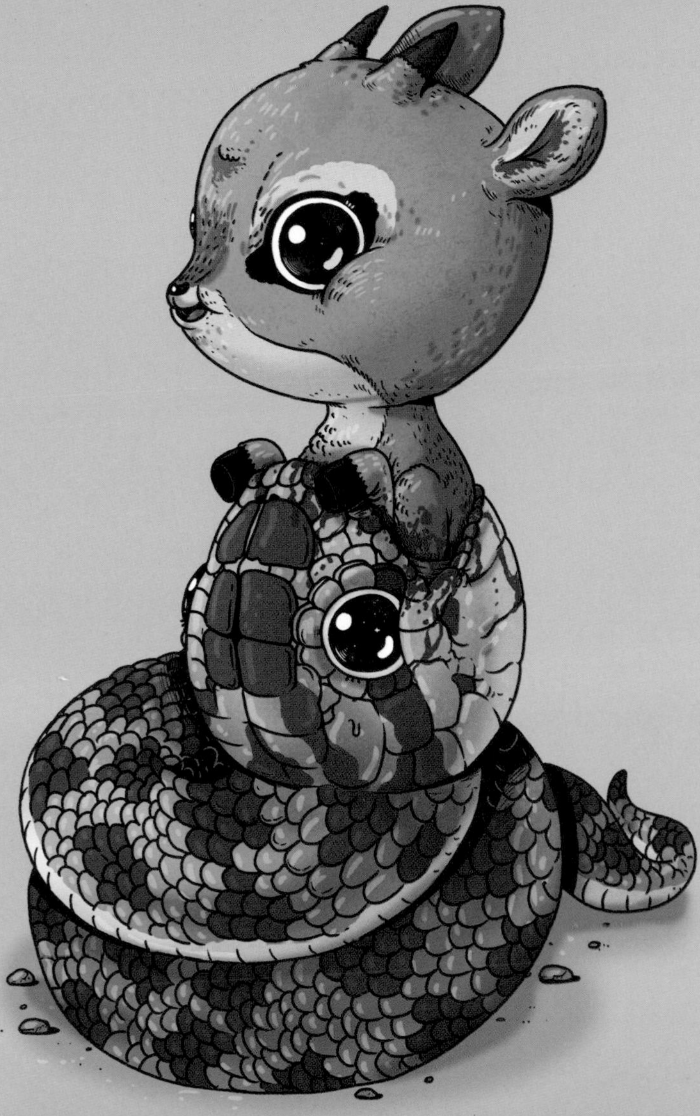

"The gypsies believe the bear to be a brother to man because he has the same body beneath his hide, because he drinks beer, because he enjoys music, and because he likes to dance."
　　　　—Ernest Hemingway


"What could be more important than a little something to eat?"
　　　　—Winnie-the-Pooh

# APPENDIX



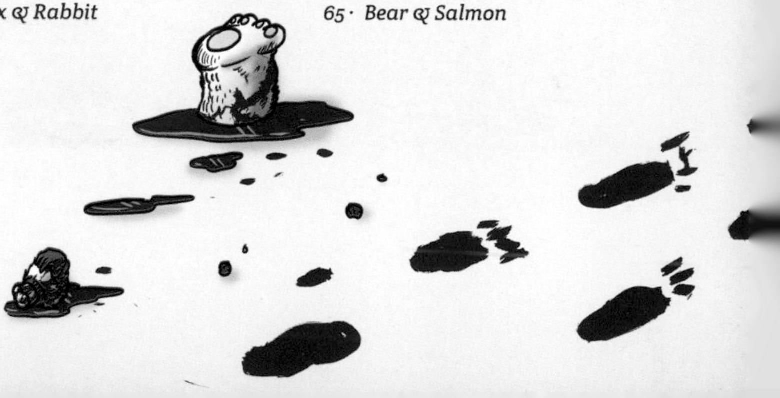

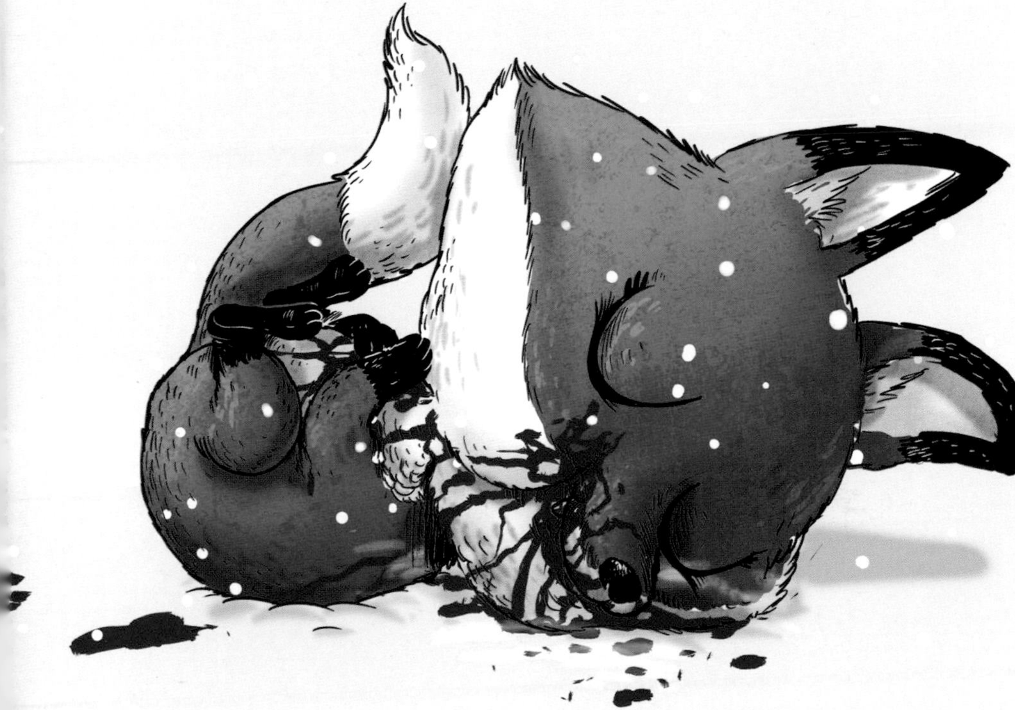

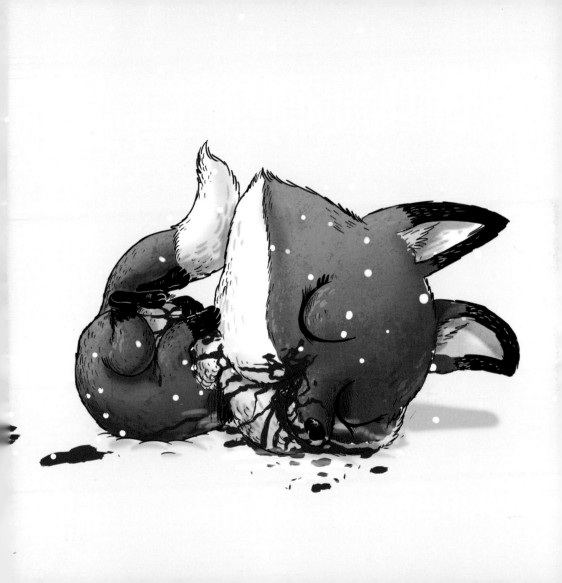

Alex Solis is an illustrator and designer, as well as a full-time husband and father.
Solis is bridging cultural gaps with the universal language of art,
as can be seen in his viral art series, including "Famous Chunkies,"
"Icons Unmasked," and the "Adorable Circle of Life."
You can see all his work online at oddworx.com.

# Also Available from Skyhorse Publishing

THE
Adorable
CIRCLE OF LIFE
ADULT COLORING BOOK
ALEX SOLIS

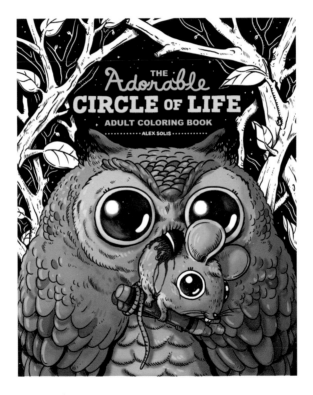

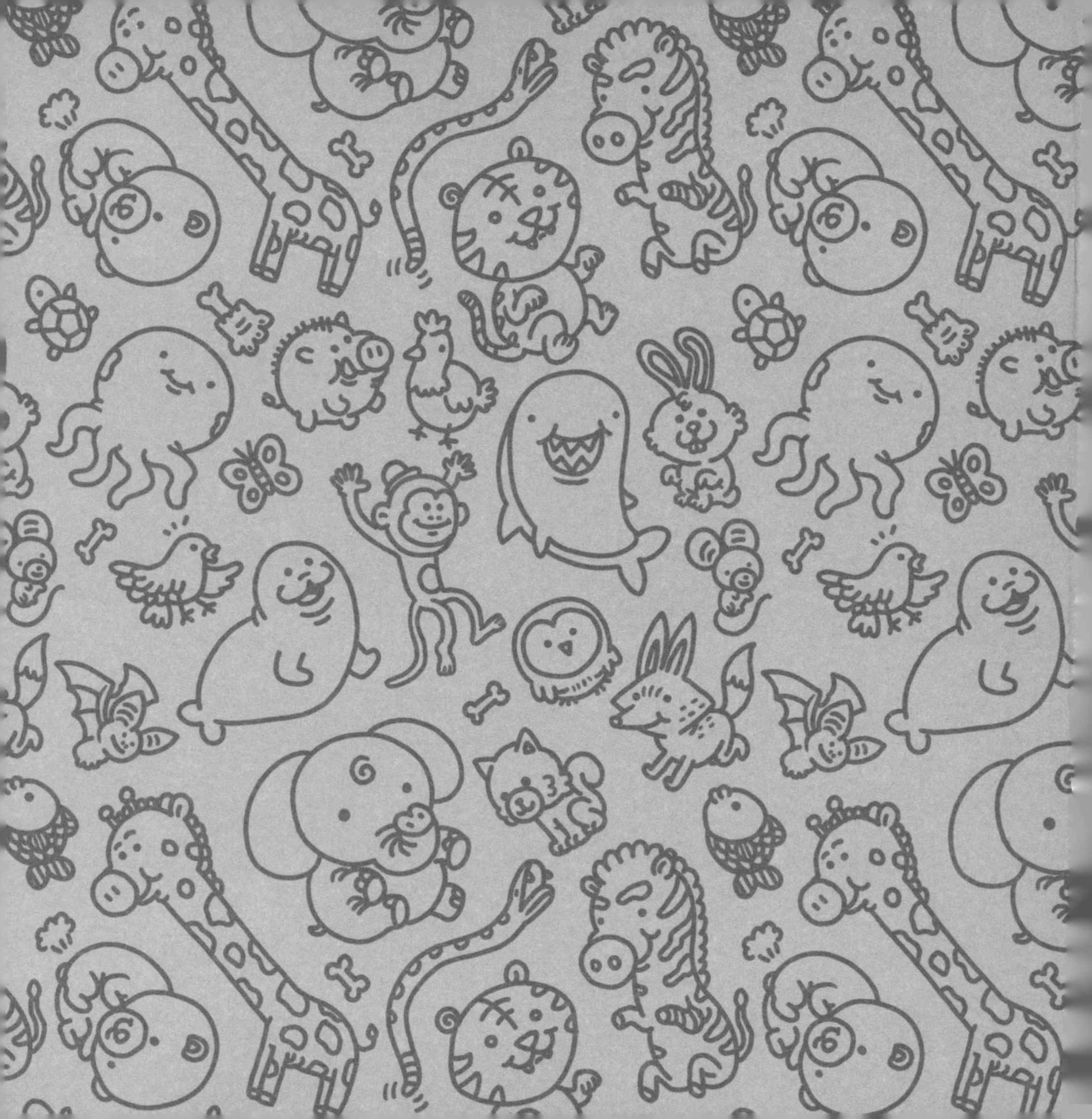